THE COMPLETE PIANO PLAYER

BOOK 2

by Kenneth Baker.

'By the end of this book, you will know more about music and you will be playing 22 popular songs, including Bright Eyes, Danny Boy, A Hard Day's Night, *and* Sailing.'

Kenneth Baker

To acces audio visit:
www.halleonardmgb.com/mylibrary

8419-4968-6777-0813

Published by
Hal Leonard

Exclusive Distributors:
Hal Leonard
7777 West Bluemound Road,
Milwaukee, WI 53213
Email: info@halleonard.com

Hal Leonard Europe Limited
42 Wigmore Street,
Marylebone, London W1U 2 RY
Email: info@halleonardeurope.com

Hal Leonard Australia Pty. Ltd.
4 Lentara Court, Cheltenham,
Victoria 9132, Australia
Email: info@halleonard.com.au

Order No. AM999966
ISBN 978-1-84938-468-1
This book © Copyright 1984, 1993, 2010 Hal Leonard

Written & arranged by Kenneth Baker.
Cover designed & art directed by Michael Bell Design.
Photography by Peter Wood.
Piano kindly loaned by Chamberlain Music.
Text pages designed by Howard Brown.
Printed in the EU.
backing tracks by Paul Honey.

www.halleonard.com

ABOUT THIS BOOK

This is the second book in *The Complete Piano Player* course. You will find it as rewarding to work through as Book 1.

As in the first book, you will learn how to play songs by famous artists and groups, including Elvis Presley, Rod Stewart, The Beatles, and others. And you will learn popular classical pieces which are a pleasure to play and to listen to.

Carefully follow the lessons, and by the end of the book you will find that you have made excellent progress in reading music and in technique. You will also be delighted to find that you have built up a fine repertoire. In all this, you are helped by the easy-to-follow text combined with numerous, clear diagrams. These are of special value to you if you are working on your own.

Remember to play regularly every day, if only for a short time. Little and often is an excellent way of making rapid progress towards becoming the complete piano player.

TO TEACHERS

The Complete Piano Player course is ideal for teaching today's students. It teaches sound technique from the beginning. At the same time, it is based on music which will keep your students interested throughout the entire course.

NEW NOTES

You start this book by learning these new notes:

A, B, C right hand
E left hand

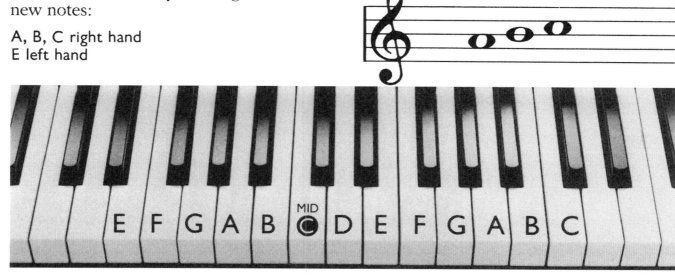

E

HOW TO FINGER THE NEW NOTES

The new notes illustrated above are beyond the range of your original five-fingered hand positions:

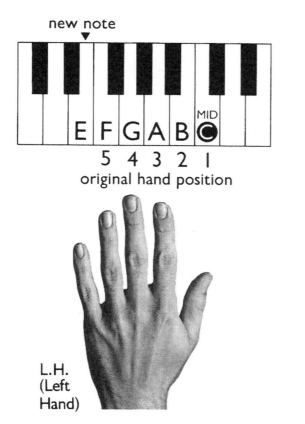

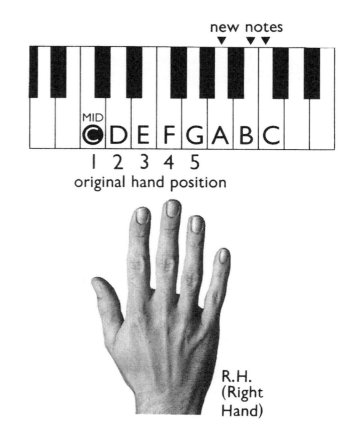

L.H. (Left Hand)

R.H. (Right Hand)

When a single new note is required, extend your hand to play it, then return to your original five finger hand position:

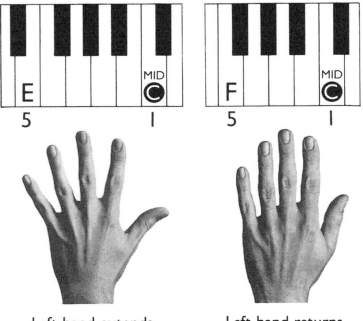

Left hand extends to play note E

Left hand returns to original five-finger position.

When several new notes are to be played consecutively take up a new five-finger position covering the new notes:

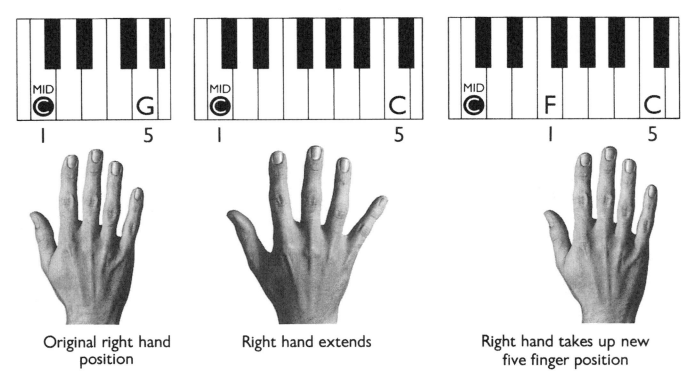

Original right hand position

Right hand extends

Right hand takes up new five finger position

I have indicated examples of both the above situations in the three pieces which follow: *Sailing, My Own True Love,* and *Wooden Heart.*

Note: From now on letter names will appear alongside new notes only.

SAILING
Words & Music: Gavin Sutherland

Remember: watch out for changes of hand positions in this and the next two pieces.

MY OWN TRUE LOVE
(TARA'S THEME)
Words: Mack David. Music: Max Steiner.

Always change hand positions smoothly

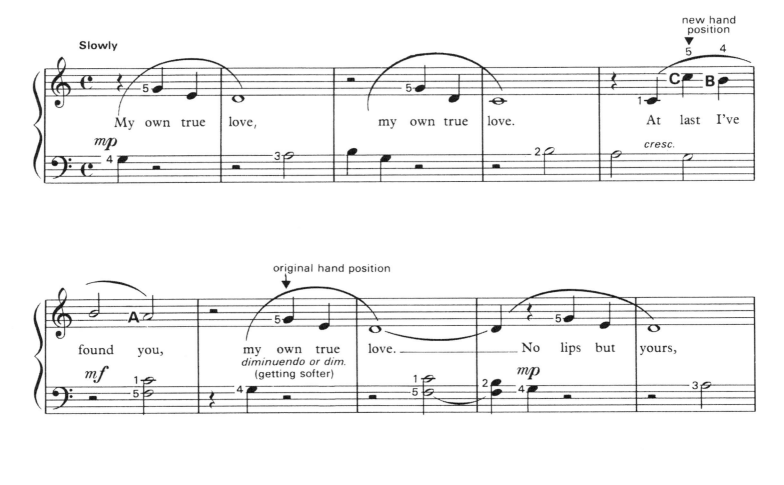

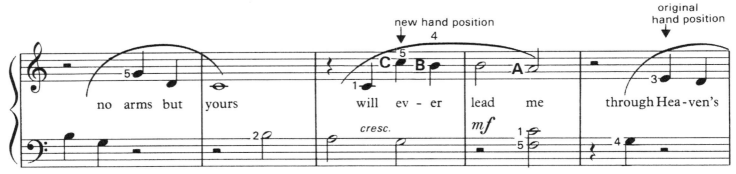

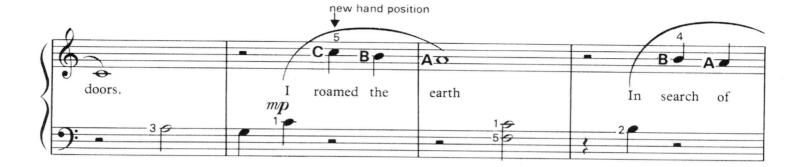

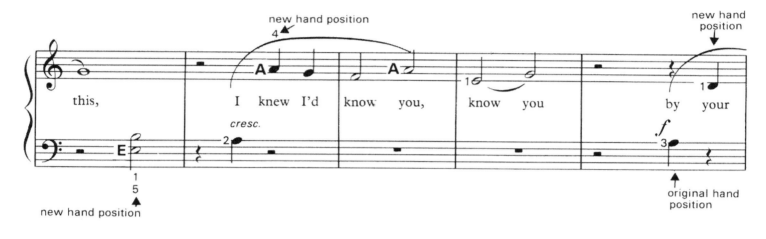

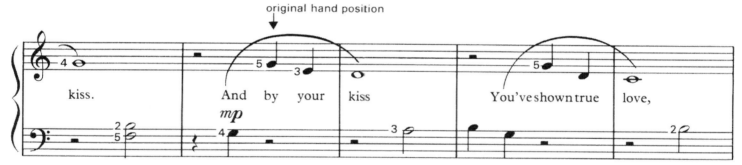

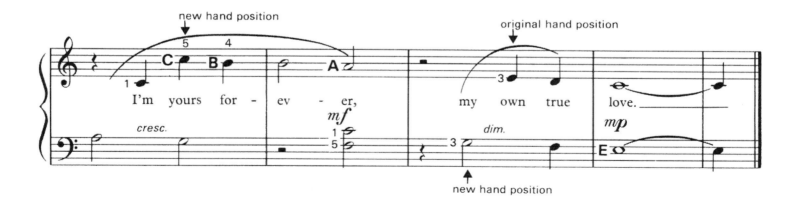

WOODEN HEART

Words & Music by Fred Wise, Ben Weisman,
Kay Twomey and Berthold Kaempfert.

Change hand positions smoothly

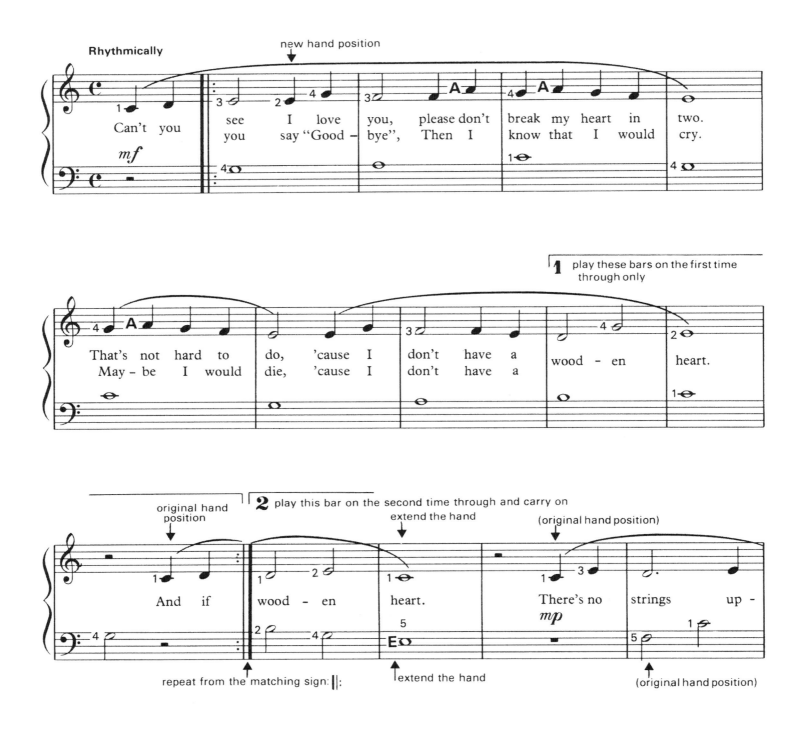

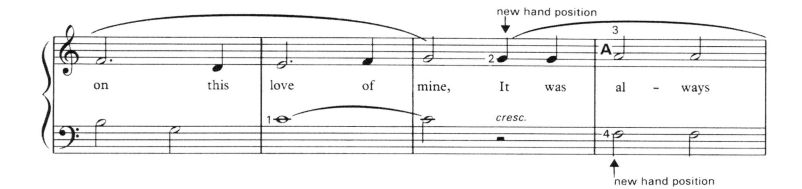

new hand position

on this love of mine, It was al - ways

new hand position

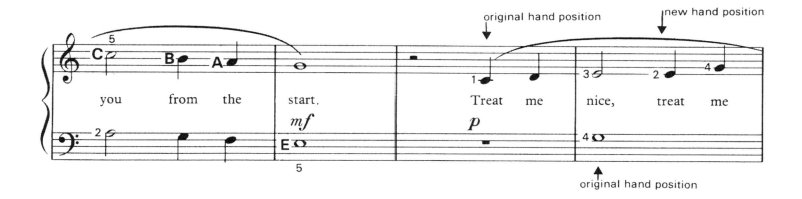

original hand position

new hand position

you from the start. Treat me nice, treat me

mf

p

original hand position

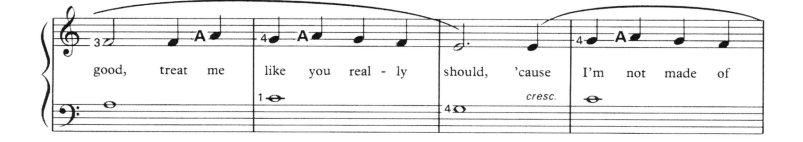

good, treat me like you real - ly should, 'cause I'm not made of

cresc.

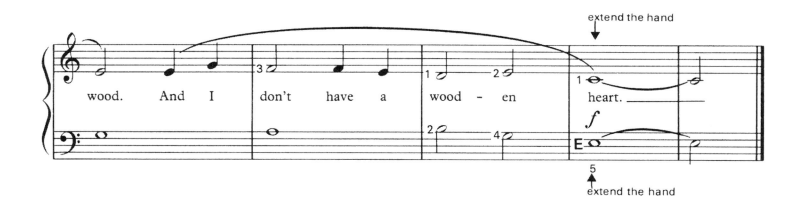

extend the hand

wood. And I don't have a wood - en heart.

f

extend the hand

From now on I leave it to you to watch
out for hand extensions and changes of
hand position. Follow the printed
fingering carefully and you can't go
wrong.

DANNY BOY

Words: Fred E. Weatherly. Music: Traditional Irish Melody

With expression

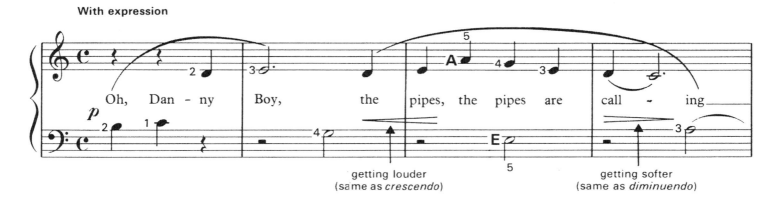

getting louder
(same as *crescendo*)

getting softer
(same as *diminuendo*)

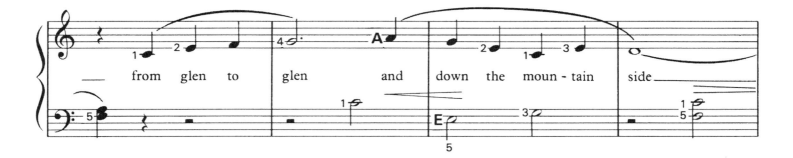

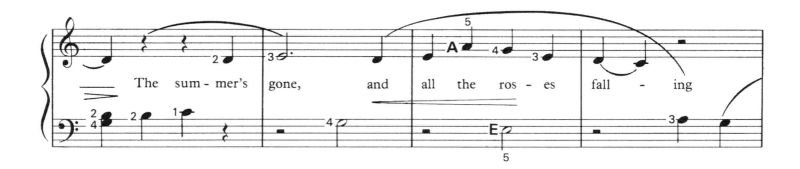

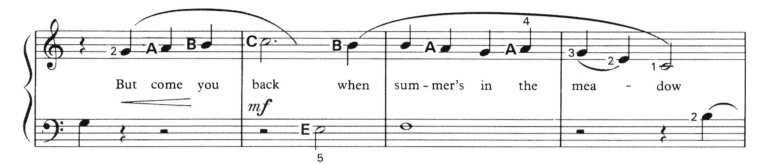

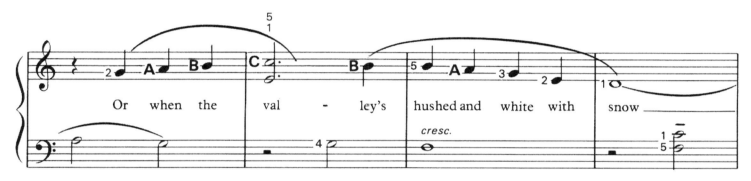

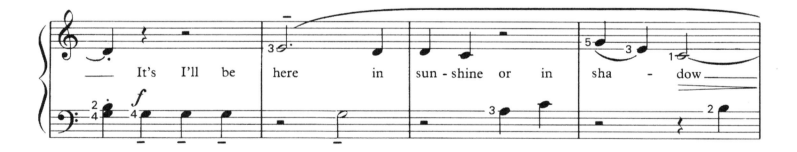

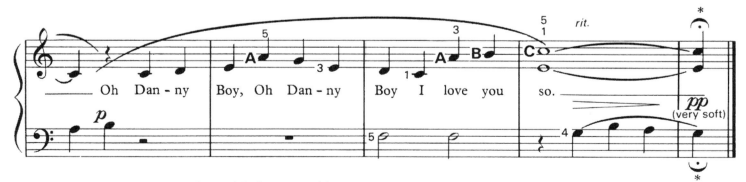

*Pause (Fermata). Hold the note(s)
longer than written (at the discretion of
the player).

SHARPS AND NATURALS

2

This sign is called a sharp: ♯ Whenever you see a sharp written against a note, it means that you must play the nearest available key to the right of that note. This key may be **black or white.**

You continue to play the sharp throughout the bar, but it is automatically cancelled at the next bar.

Another way of cancelling a sharp is by writing a 'natural' sign against the note. The natural sign is written like this: ♮ For an example of the use of a natural sign, see bar 15 of *Puff The Magic Dragon*.

The most commonly used sharp is:

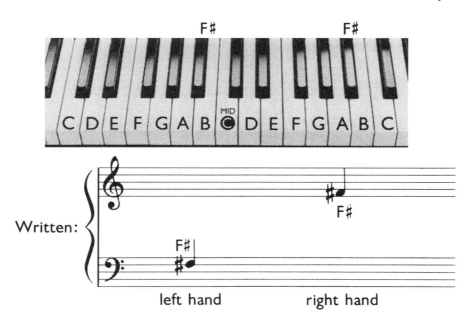

Written:

left hand   right hand

EXAMPLES OF OTHER SHARPS

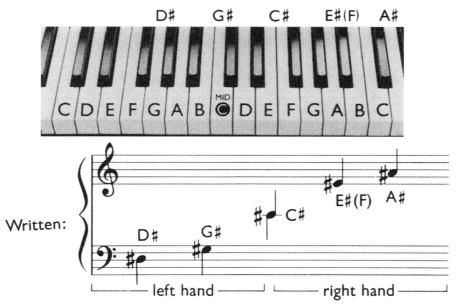

Written:

Notice that E♯ and F are exactly the same note. Sometimes it is more convenient to call F 'E♯'

PUFF (THE MAGIC DRAGON)

Words & Music by: Peter Yarrow and Leonard Lipton

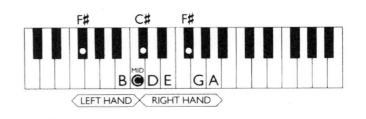

Watch out for 'sharp' notes in this piece. Remember to return to 'natural' notes.

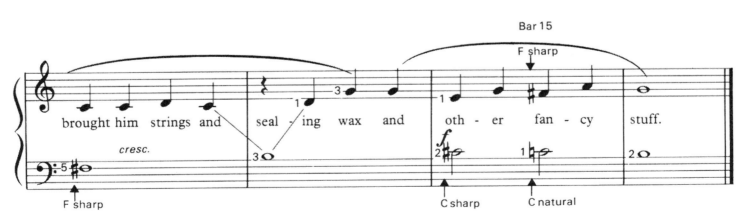

METRONOME MARKS

3

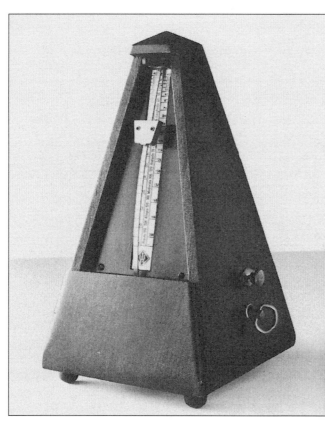

clockwork metronome

electronic metronome

A metronome is an instrument which indicates the speed of a piece of music.

The metronome mark: ♩= 176 at the beginning of the next piece means that there are to be 176 Crotchets (quarter notes) a minute (rather fast).
Set the pendulum to 176 and the instrument will "tick" at the correct speed.
Don't leave the metronome running during your piece. Once you have the "feel" of the correct speed, switch off.

CHORD SYMBOLS

From now on chord symbols will be included in all pieces. These symbols are intended for other instrumentalists, such as guitarists, who may wish to accompany you.

LAUGHING SAMBA
Words: Benny Meroff & Anne Spear.
Music: Vincent Rizzo & George Johnson.

Brightly ♩ = 176

C			Dm

Fun - ny   lit - tle   "Song - a",   some - thing   like   a   Con - ga,
Ev' - ry   one   can   do   it,   there   is   noth - ing   to   it,

mf

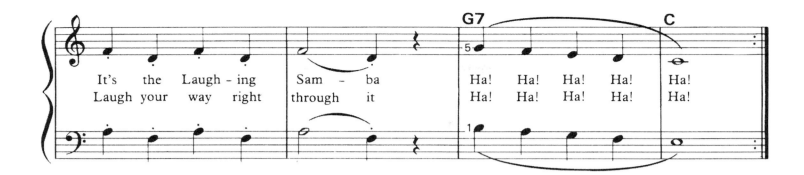

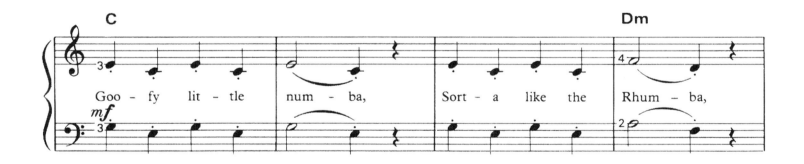

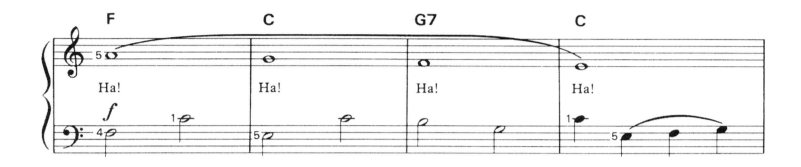

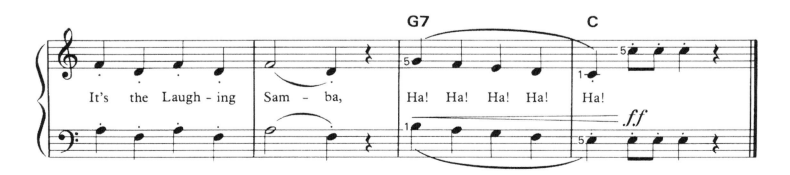

FLATS

4

A flat: ♭ against a note means play the nearest available key (black or white) to the left of that note.

The flat continues through the bar but is cancelled automatically at the next bar.

A 'natural': ♮ may also be used to cancel a flat.

The most commonly used flat is:

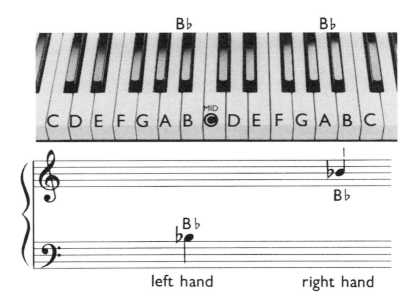

left hand   right hand

EXAMPLES OF OTHER FLATS

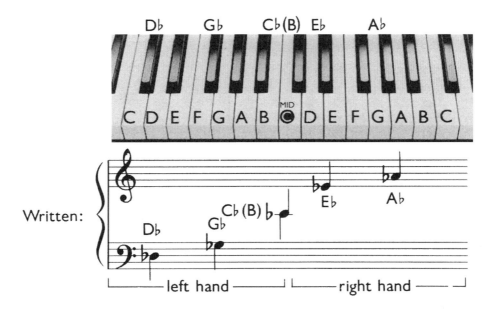

Written:

left hand   right hand

Notice that C♮ and B are exactly the same note. Sometimes it is more convenient to call B 'C♭'

LET HIM GO, LET HIM TARRY

Traditional

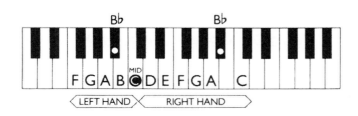

Watch out for 'flat' notes in this and the following piece. Remember to return to 'natural' notes.

THE WINNER TAKES IT ALL

Words & Music: Benny Andersson & Bjorn Ulvaeus

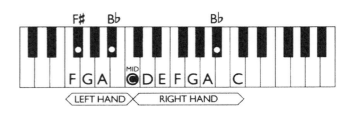

With a precise rhythm ♩ = 92

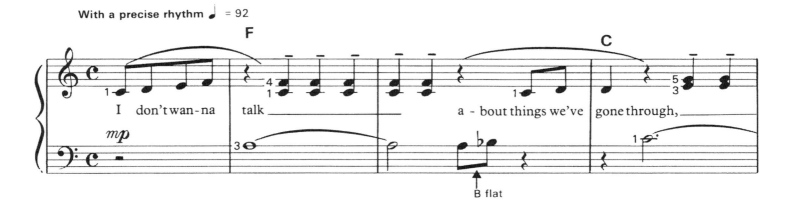

I don't wan-na talk a - bout things we've gone through,

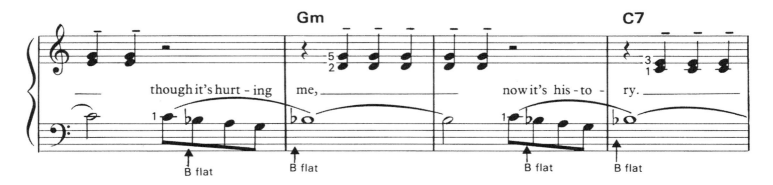

though it's hurt-ing me, now it's his-to-ry.

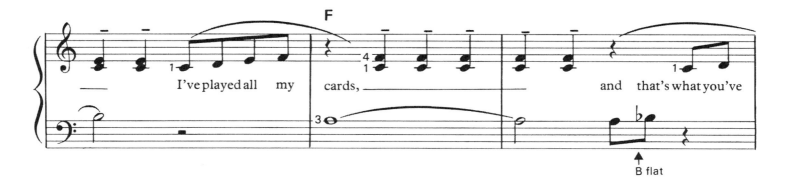

I've played all my cards, and that's what you've

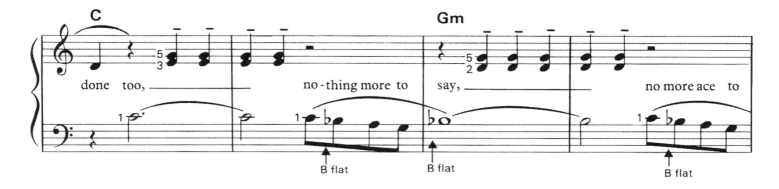

done too, no-thing more to say, no more ace to

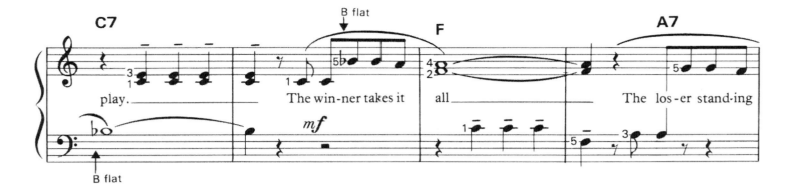

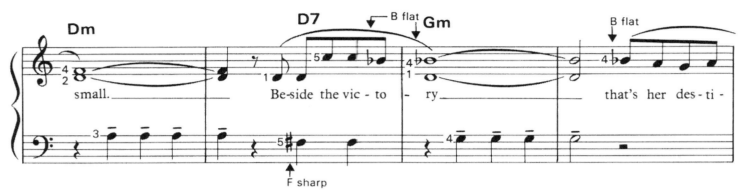

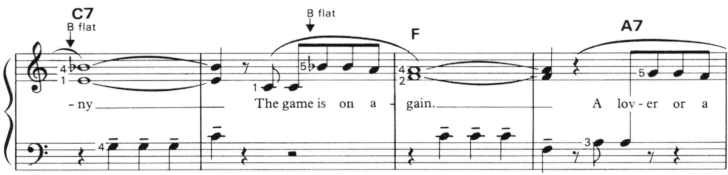

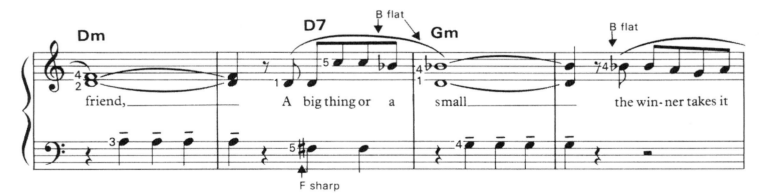

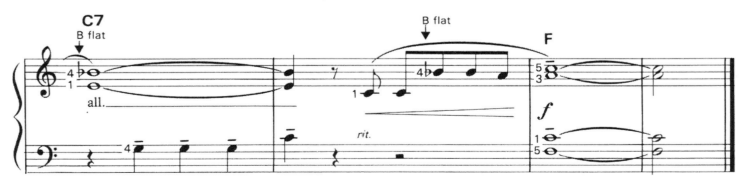

NEW NOTES

5 You are now going to learn a famous song by The Beatles. But before you tackle it, here are two new notes:

D for right hand
D for left hand

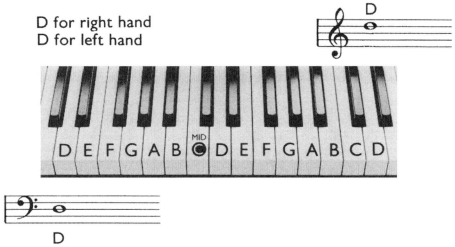

Both these notes – which are shown above – occur in your new piece, so make sure you know them.

A HARD DAY'S NIGHT
Words & Music: John Lennon and Paul McCartney

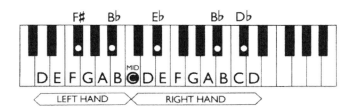

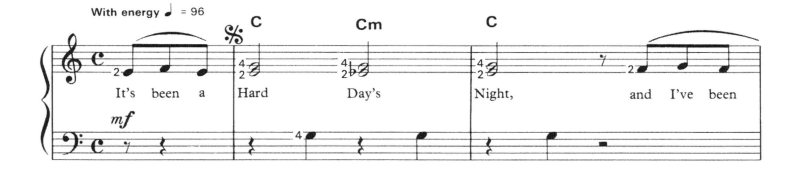

Night, I should be sleep - ing like a log_____ But when I

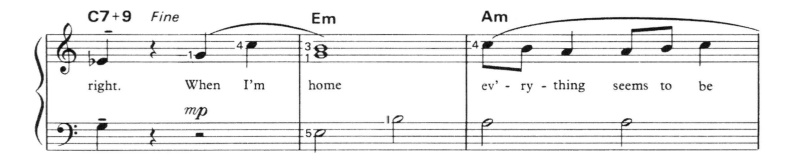

get home to you, I find the things that you do will make me feel_____ all _____

right. When I'm home ev' - ry - thing seems to be

right_____ when I'm home

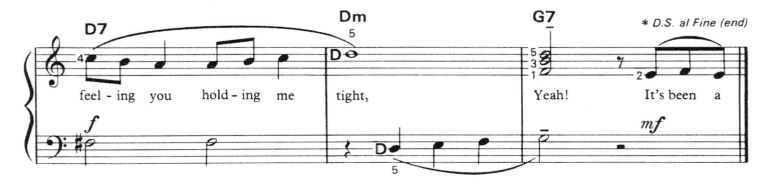

feel - ing you hold - ing me tight, Yeah! It's been a

*Dal Segno al Fine. 'From the sign to the end'. Go back to the sign 𝄋 and continue playing until 'Fine' (the end of the piece).

SCALE OF C, KEY OF C, PASSING NOTES

6

A 'Scale' is a succession of adjoining notes ascending or descending.

The 'Scale of C (Major)' requires no black notes:

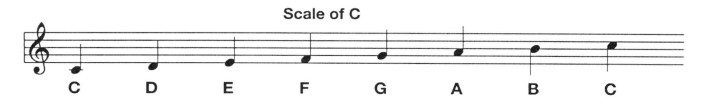

Scale of C

C D E F G A B C

When the notes used in a piece of music are all taken from the Scale of C, the piece is said to be in the 'Key of C'.

PASSING NOTES

However, a piece of music in C could use notes which are not in the Scale of C. If these notes are brief they are called 'passing notes'. Passing notes are of a temporary nature only and do not affect the overall key.

In the following piece, "He'll Have To Go", look out for 'passing notes' in both hands.

HE'LL HAVE TO GO

Words & Music: Joe Allison & Audrey Allison

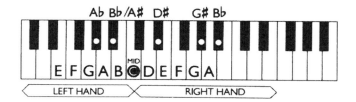

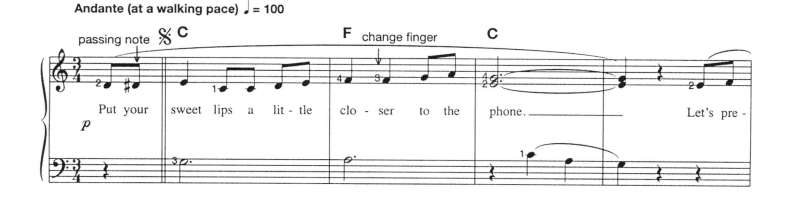

Andante (at a walking pace) ♩ = 100

passing note   C   F change finger   C

Put your | sweet lips a lit - tle | clo - ser to the | phone. ____ | Let's pre -

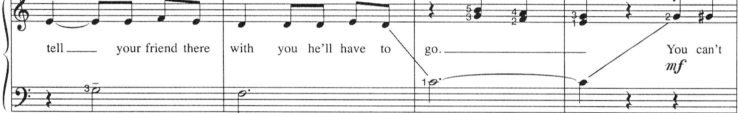

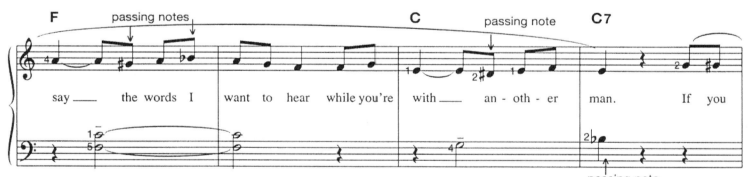

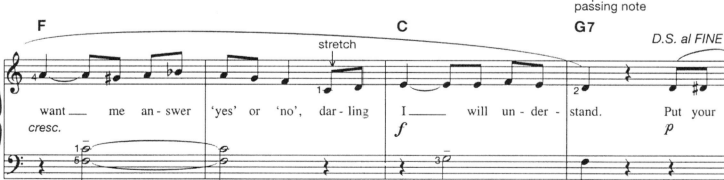

COMMON TIME AND
CUT COMMON TIME (ALLA BREVE)

7

The sign **C** stands for $\frac{4}{4}$ time, that is, there are four crotchets (or quarter notes) to the bar. $\frac{4}{4}$ is also known as 'Common Time'.

The sign **₵** stands for $\frac{2}{2}$ time, that is, there are two minims (or half notes) to the bar. $\frac{2}{2}$ time is also known as 'Cut Common Time', or Alla Breve.

Pieces written in Cut Common Time have a distinct feel of two in a bar, and they tend to be faster than those written in Common Time.

THOSE LAZY, HAZY, CRAZY DAYS OF SUMMER
Words: Charles Tobias. Music: Hans Carste

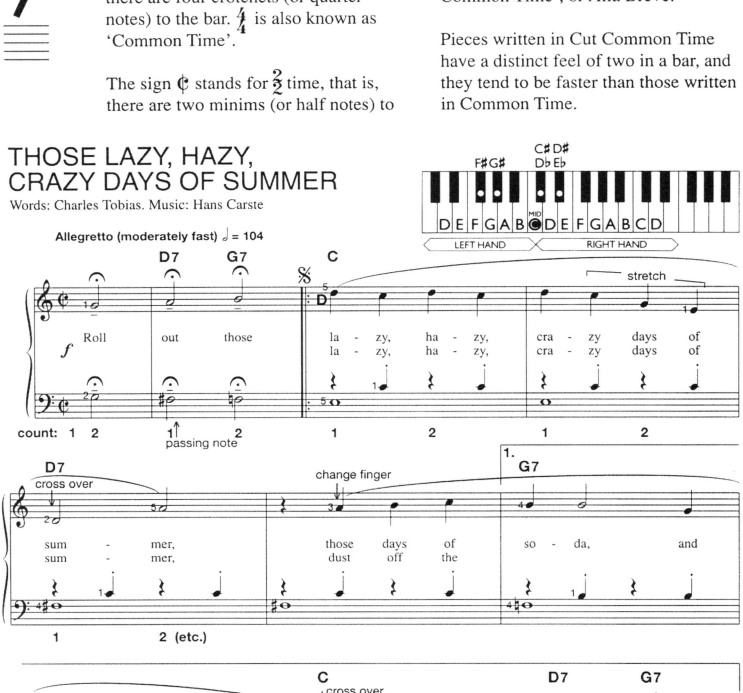

Allegretto (moderately fast) ♩ = 104

count: 1 2 | 1 2 | 1 | 2 | 1 | 2

passing note

Roll out those la - zy, ha - zy, cra - zy days of summer,

la - zy, ha - zy, cra - zy days of summer,

cross over

change finger

1.

sum - mer, those days of so - da, and

dust off the

1 2 (etc.)

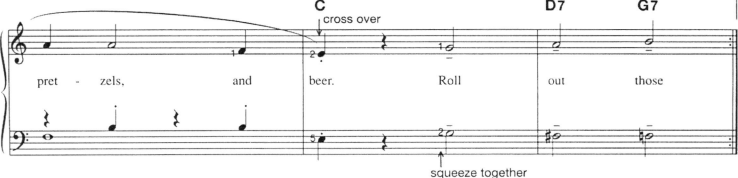

pret - zels, and beer. Roll out those

squeeze together

26

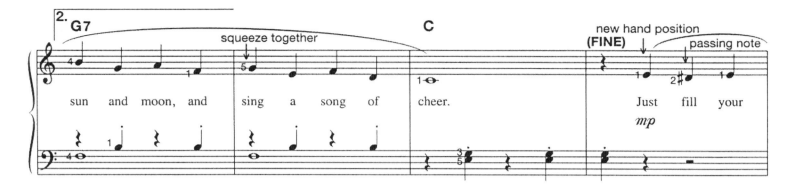

2. **G7** squeeze together **C** new hand position **(FINE)** passing note

sun and moon, and sing a song of cheer. Just fill your

mp

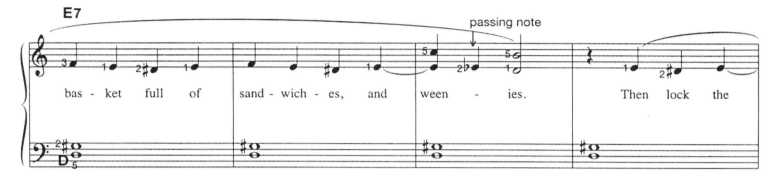

E7 passing note

bas - ket full of sand - wich - es, and ween - ies. Then lock the

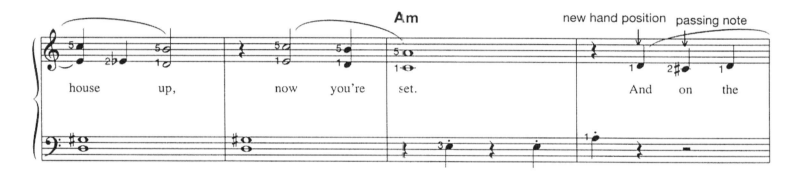

Am new hand position passing note

house up, now you're set. And on the

D7 passing note new hand position

beach you'll see the girls in their bi - ki - nis, as cute as

cresc.

D.S. (with Repeat) al FINE

G7 new hand position **D7** **G7**

e - ver, but they nev - er get 'em wet! Roll out those

f

SCALE OF F, KEY OF F, KEY SIGNATURE

8

Read lesson 6 again to refresh your memory about Scales, Keys, and Passing Notes.

The Key of F (Major) comes from the Scale of F (Major), which has one black note: B flat.

Scale of F

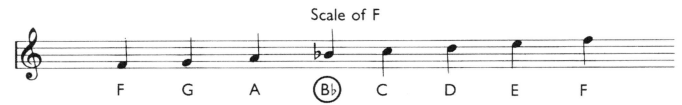

F G A (B♭) C D E F

Pieces which are written in the Key of F (major) use the notes from the scale of the same name, although the piece may also include some passing notes.

When a piece is written in the key of F (major), it is necessary to indicate the B flats at the beginning of the piece, like this:

Key of F major

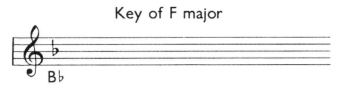

B♭

This is called the 'Key Signature'. It tells you that whenever you see the note B, you play it as B flat.

Under The Bridges Of Paris, which you are going to play now, is in the Key of F major, as you can see from the key signature.

Remember: you play all B's as B flats wherever they fall on the keyboard.

A REMINDER ABOUT NATURALS

A 'natural' sign: ♮ cancels a sharp or flat. The natural continues through the bar, but at the next bar everything reverts to normal.

UNDER THE BRIDGES OF PARIS
(SOUS LES PONTS DE PARIS)
Music: Vincent Scotto. English lyric: Dorcas Cochran.
French lyric: J. Rodor.

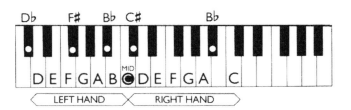

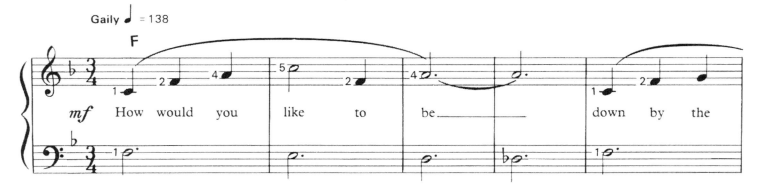

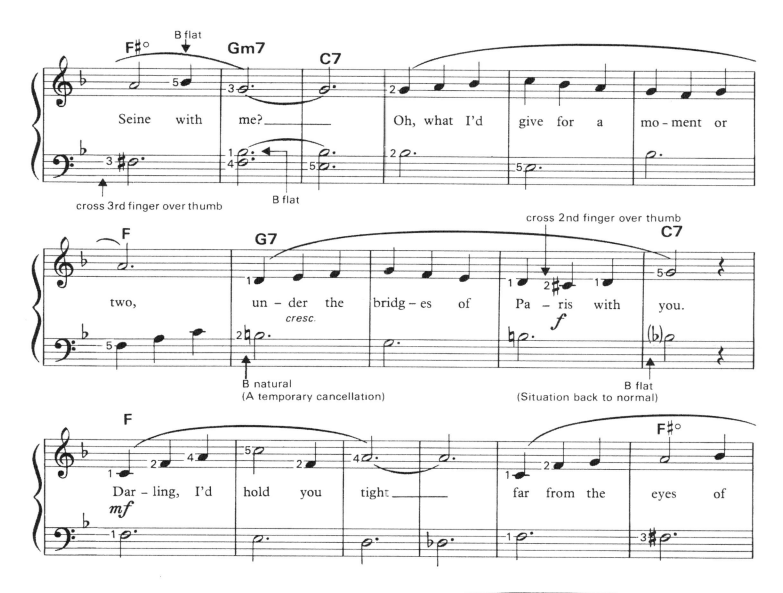

Seine with me? Oh, what I'd give for a mo-ment or

cross 3rd finger over thumb   B flat

two, un-der the bridg-es of Pa-ris with you.

cross 2nd finger over thumb

cresc.

B natural
(A temporary cancellation)

B flat
(Situation back to normal)

Dar - ling, I'd hold you tight far from the eyes of

mf

night Un - der the bridg—es of Pa - ris with

cresc.

you, I'd make your dreams come true.

f

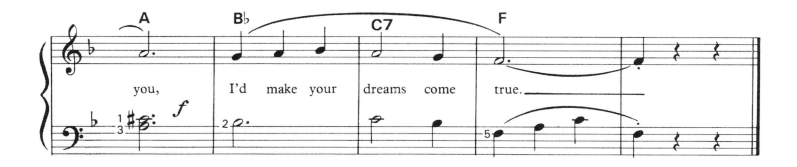

LIEBESTRÄUME

By: Franz Liszt

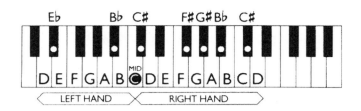

Remember: This solo is in F major.
Play all B's as B flats, unless
instructed otherwise.

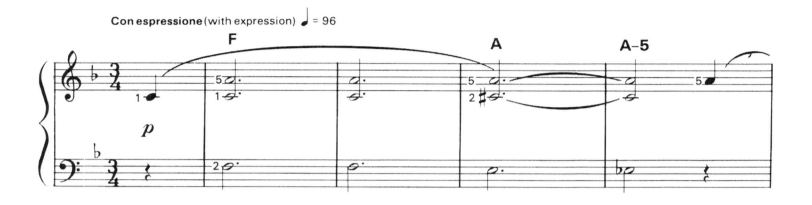

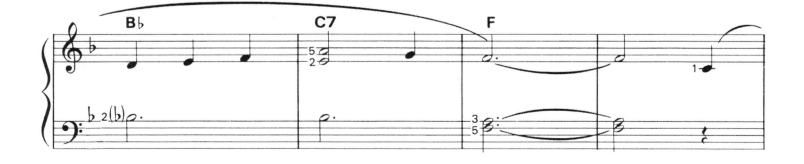

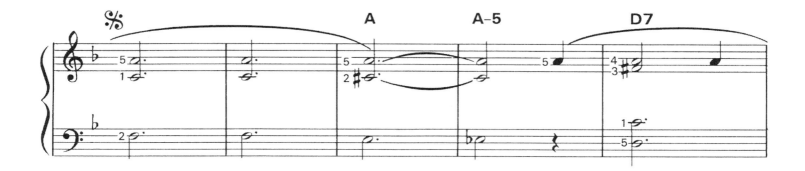

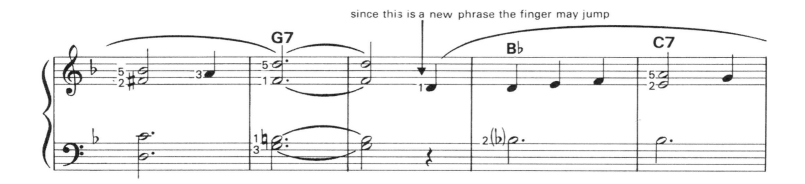

since this is a new phrase the finger may jump

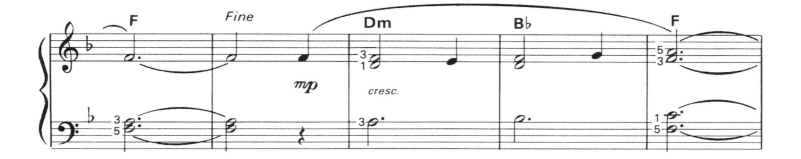

change to 3rd finger
on A

*In Time i.e. pick up the original speed

BRIGHT EYES

Words & Music: Mike Batt

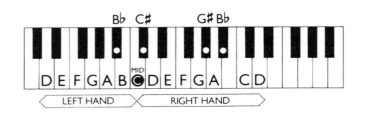

**Remember: All B's are to be played as
B flats, unless instructed otherwise.**

Is it a kind of a dream ____
fog a-long the hor-i-zon,

Float-ing out on the
Cold sound in the ____

tide ____
air ____

Fol-low-ing the riv-er of
no-bo-dy ev-er knows

death down-stream
when you go

Oh is it a
And where do you

dream? ____

There's a

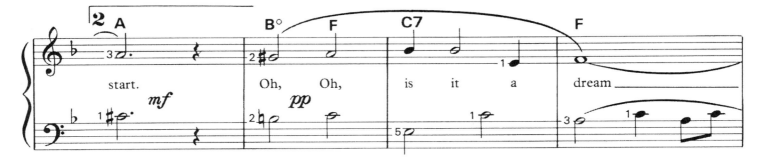

start.

Oh, Oh,

is it a

dream ____

*Repeat Marking. Since there is no
matching Repeat Sign to go back to,
repeat from the beginning of the piece.

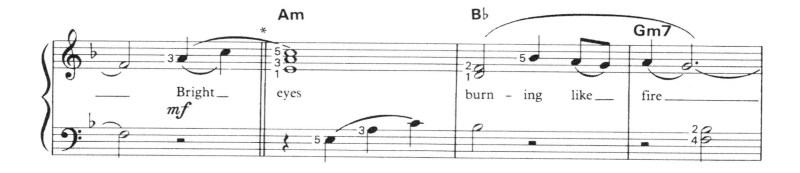

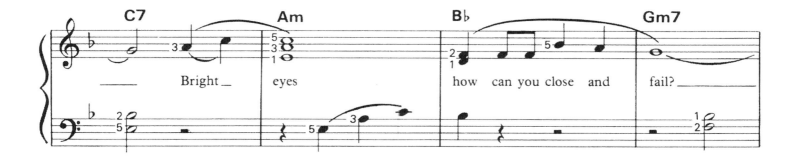

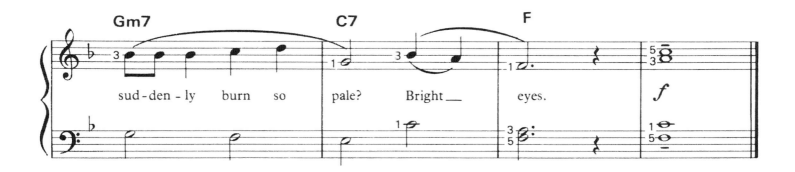

*Section Lines. End of one Section of the piece and the beginning of another.

NEW NOTES

9

Before tackling the next two pieces, here are some new notes for you to learn. Make sure that you can recognise them as soon as you see them, by practising them a few times:

E, F for right hand
C for left hand

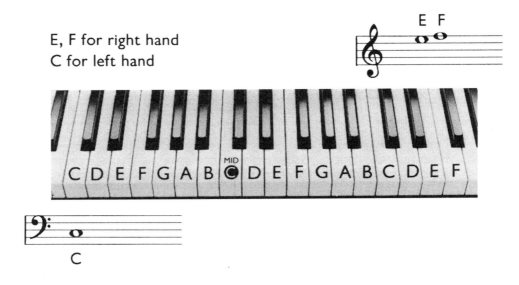

PLAISIR D'AMOUR

Words & Music: Giovanni Paolo Martini

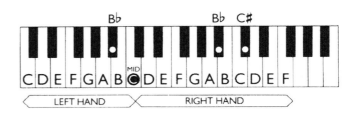

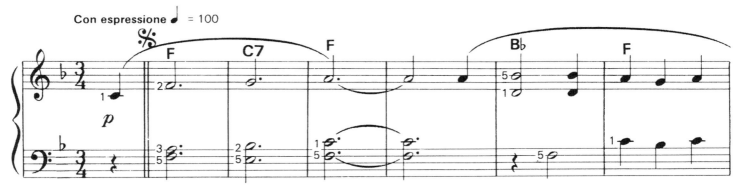

Con espressione ♩ = 100

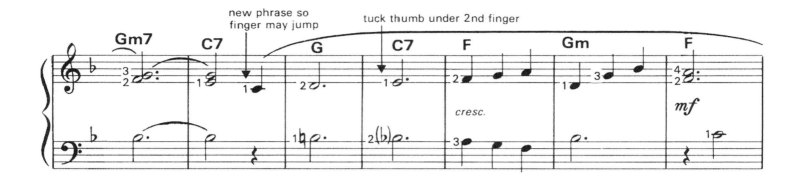

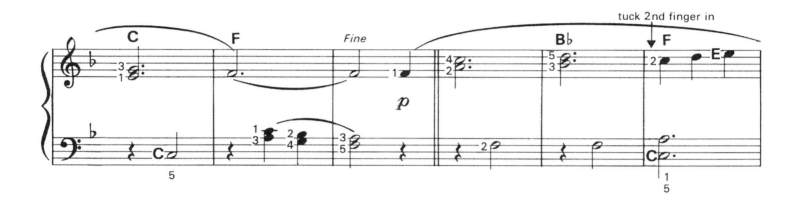

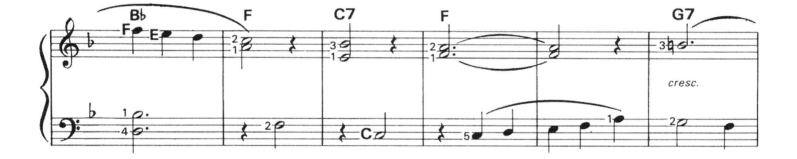

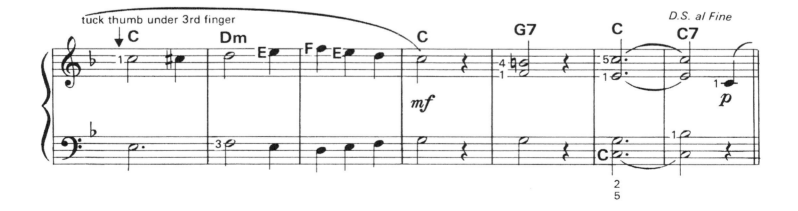

TAKE ME HOME, COUNTRY ROADS

Words & Music: Bill Danoff,
Taffy Nivert and John Denver

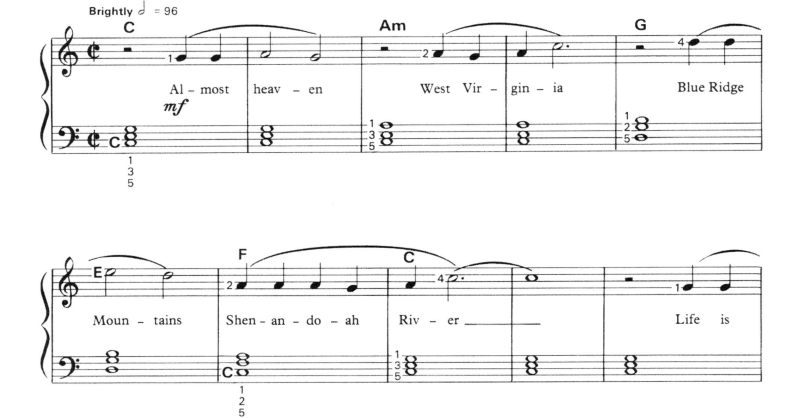

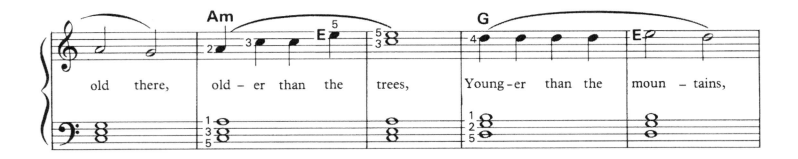

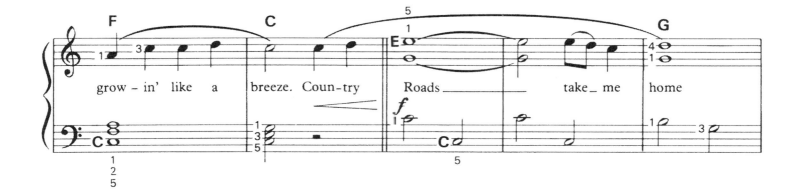

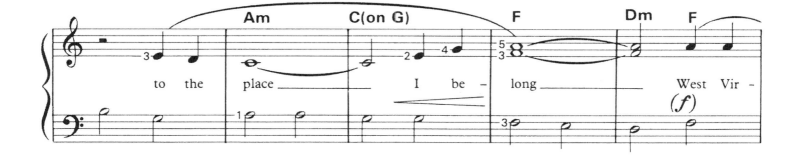

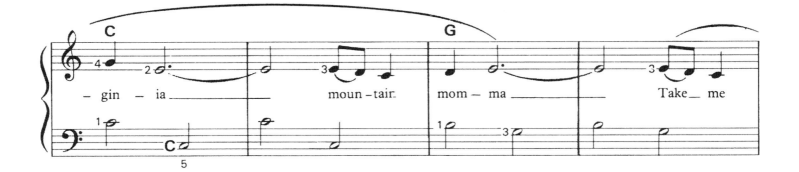

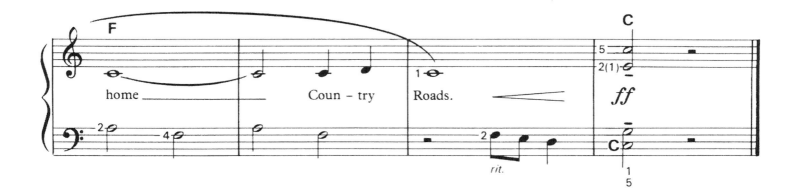

DOTTED CROTCHET
(DOTTED QUARTER NOTE)

10

A dot after a note increases its value by one half. When you apply this principle to a crotchet (quarter note) you get:

♩ crotchet (quarter note) = 1 beat

♩· dotted crotchet (dotted quarter note) = 1½ beats

A dotted crotchet (1½ beats) is almost always accompanied by a single quaver (½ beat), making two full crotchet beats in all:

♩· ♪ 1½ beats + ½ beat Total: 2 beats

or:

♪ ♩· ½ beat + 1½ beats Total: 2 beats

The first of these dotted crotchet/quaver combinations: ♩· ♪ appears frequently in the piece that follows.
It is counted like this:

SILENT NIGHT

count: 1   2 and 3   1   2   3

Pick a suitable speed for your basic crotchet beat **and be sure to maintain the same speed throughout the piece.**

BAR 1
- Play 'G' on beat 1 and let the sound continue as you count beat 2.
- Play 'A' on the 'and' between beats 2 and 3.
- Play 'G' on beat 3.

BAR 2
- Play 'E' on beat 1 and let the sound continue through beats 2 and 3.

Continue similarly through the piece.

LEFT HAND MELODY

Notice that during Bars 9-16 of *Silent Night* the Left Hand plays the melody. Increase the volume of the Left Hand at this point so that the melody can be heard clearly.

SILENT NIGHT

Words & Music: Joseph Mohr and Franz Gruber

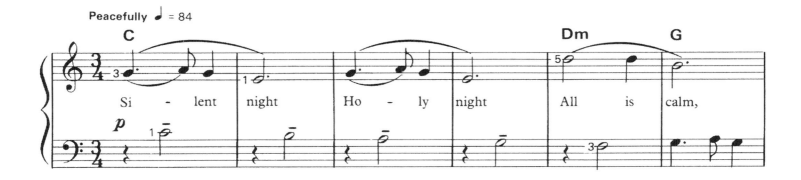

cross 3rd finger over thumb

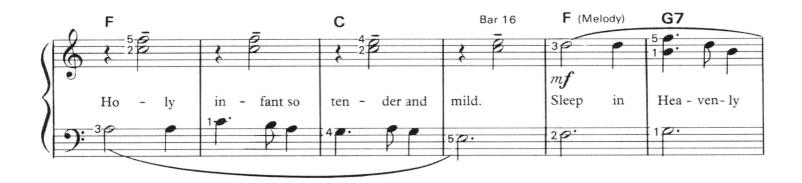

DOTTED CROTCHET
(DOTTED QUARTER NOTE)-2

The next song features the second of our dotted crotchet/quaver combinations.

This time the quaver is played first:

♪ ♩. ½ beat + 1½ beats Total: 2 beats

Count this figure like this:

GUANTANAMERA

BAR 1   BAR 3   (etc)

Count: 1   2 and 3 and 4   1 2 3 and 4 and   1   2 and 3 and 4

Maintain a regular crotchet (quarter note) beat throughout. It helps to tap your foot on the main beat.

BAR 1
- Play 'D' and 'F' together on beat 1.
- Play the same on beat 2.
- Play the same on the 'and' between beats 2 and 3.
- Play the same on beat 3.
- Play the same on the 'and' between beats 3 and 4.
- Let the sound continue through beat 4.

BAR 3
- Play 'C' on beat 1.
- Play 'D' on beat 2.
- Play 'A' on the 'and' between beats 2 and 3.
- Play 'C' on beat 3.
- Play 'C' on the 'and' between beats 3 and 4.
- Let the sound continue through beat 4.

Continue like this through the piece.

GUANTANAMERA

Words by: Jose Marti.
Music adaptation by: Hector Angulo and Pete Seeger.

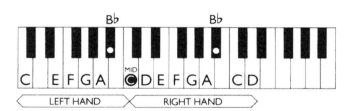

With a gentle rhythm ♩ = 92

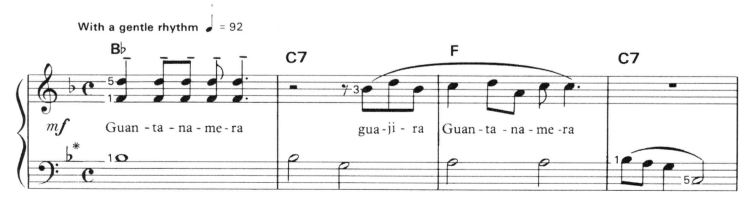

mf

Guan - ta - na - me - ra   gua - ji - ra   Guan - ta - na - me - ra

TEACHERS: * The flat has been put here for the moment because the pupil has not been taught the lower 'B' note. The normal F major key signature appears in Book 3 page 12.

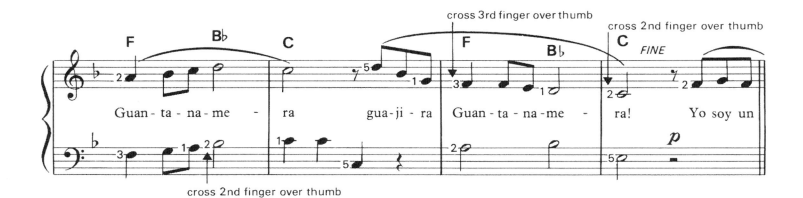

*Da Capo al Fine 'From the beginning to
the end'. Go back to the beginning of the
piece and continue playing until 'Fine'
(the end of the piece).

The next piece makes use of both the
♩.♪ and ♪ ♩. dotted crotchet/quaver
combinations.

BY THE TIME I GET TO PHOENIX

Words & Music: Jim Webb

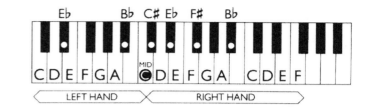

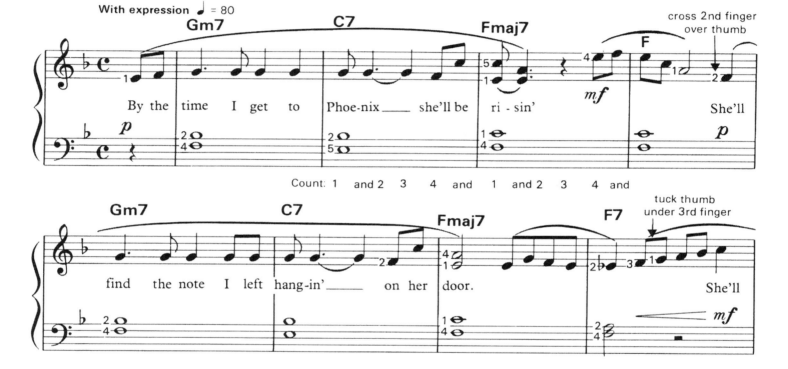

Count: 1 and 2 3 4 and 1 and 2 3 4 and

new bar, so "E" natural

WRIST STACCATO

12

Hand in position to strike

Down stroke

Up stroke

Learning the following piece will give you practice in wrist staccato. After each note let your hand spring up from your wrist **without moving your arm.**

Keep your wrist flexible and you will always feel comfortable when using this technique.

WILLIAM TELL OVERTURE
(THEME FROM)

By: Gioacchino Rossini

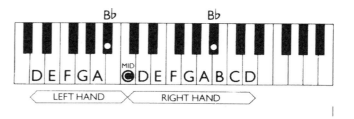

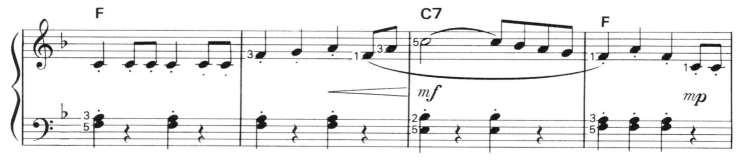

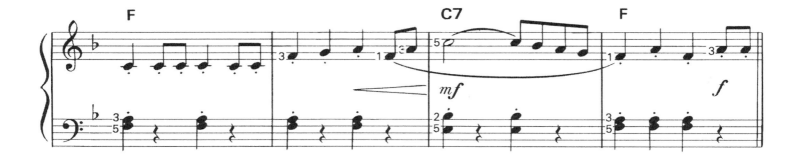

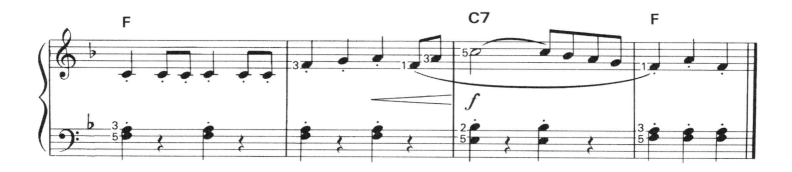

TWO TUNES WITH ONE HAND

13

Often in a piece of piano music there is a second tune accompanying the main tune. There may even be more than one secondary tune. These secondary tunes can be complete 'counter' melodies, or just short, melodic fragments put in to enhance the main melody. This is similar to choral music, where the singers are singing different tunes (or 'parts'), the whole blending together to create the 'harmony'.

On the piano, these secondary 'parts' tend to occur below, that is lower than, the main melody. Two parts are often played by one hand.

Look at bars 6 and 7 and bars 22, 23 and 24 of the following song. You will see examples of two different tunes, or parts, played by the right hand. Hold all lower notes for their full value and finger 'legato' in order to bring out the lower parts.

WHAT KIND OF FOOL AM I
Words & Music: Leslie Bricusse & Anthony Newley

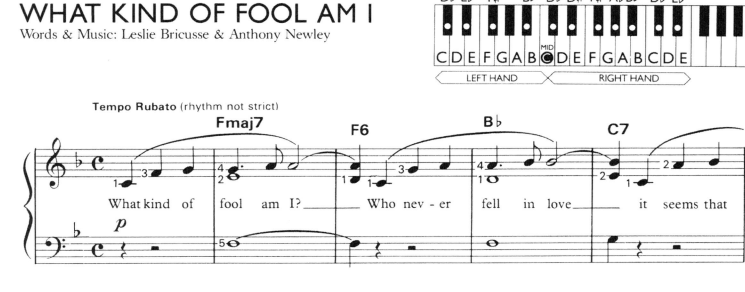

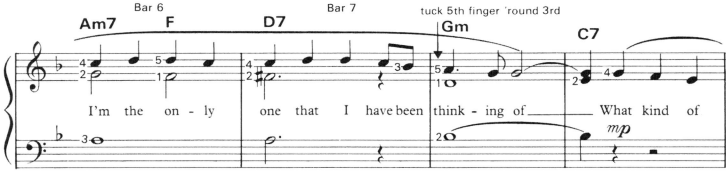

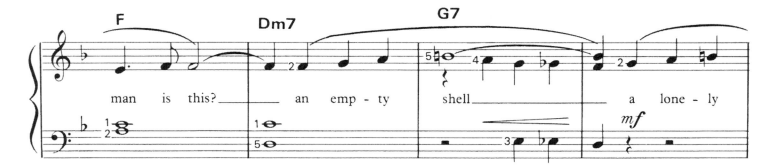

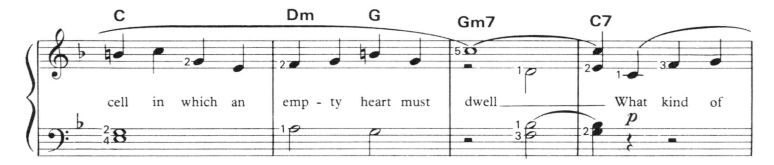

cell in which an emp - ty heart must dwell_____ What kind of

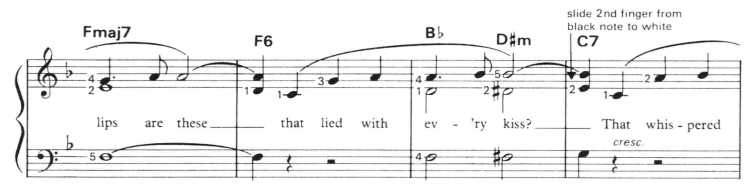

slide 2nd finger from black note to white

lips are these_____ that lied with ev - 'ry kiss?_____ That whis - pered

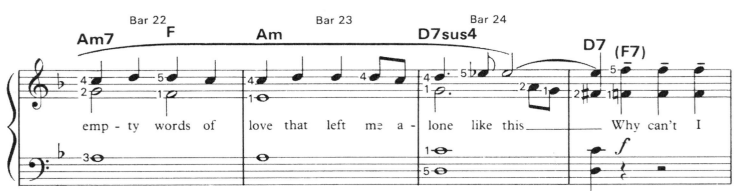

emp - ty words of love that left me a - lone like this_____ Why can't I

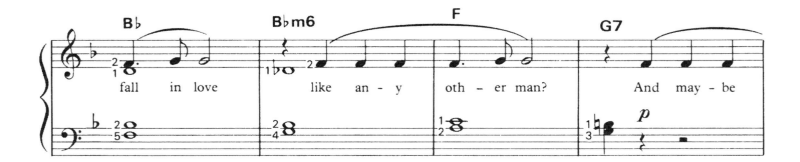

fall in love like an - y oth - er man? And may - be

then I'll know what kind of fool I am.

tuck thumb under 2nd finger

LAST WORD

Congratulations on reaching the end of Book 2 of The Complete Piano Player!

In Book Three you will be:
- Learning new notes
- Playing in different keys
- Discovering new left hand styles and rhythms
- Developing your piano technique

Till then your last song in this book is:

LET IT BE

Words & Music: John Lennon & Paul McCartney